Parental Guidance Ratings

by Casie Hermansson

Content Consultant
Prof. Clay Calvert
Director, Marion B. Brechner First Amendment Project
University of Florida

CORE
LIBRARY

Published by ABDO Publishing Company, PO Box 398166, Minneapolis, MN 55439. Copyright © 2013 by Abdo Consulting Group, Inc. International copyrights reserved in all countries. No part of this book may be reproduced in any form without written permission from the publisher. The Core Library™ is a trademark and logo of ABDO Publishing Company.

Printed in the United States of America,
North Mankato, Minnesota
102012
012013

Editor: Karen Latchana Kenney
Series Designer: Becky Daum

Cataloging-in-Publication Data
Hermansson, Casie.
 Parental guidance ratings / Casie Hermansson.
   p. cm. -- (Hot topics in media)
Includes index.
ISBN 978-1-61783-734-0
1. Motion pictures--Ratings. 2. Electronic games--Age suitability ratings.
3. Television programs--Ratings. I. Title.
302.23--dc14

                                        2012946379

Photo Credits: Paul Sakuma/AP Images, cover, title, 35; Warner Bros. Pictures/Photofest, 4; Damian Dovarganes/AP Images, 7; Jeff Chiu/ AP Images, 8; Khakimullin Aleksandr/Shutterstock Images, 11; Getty Images, 12, 23; Bettman/Corbis/AP Images, 15; AP Images, 17, 28; Lawrence Lucier/Getty Images, 20; Doug Mills/AP Images, 25; Photoroller/ Shutterstock Images, 31; PRNewsFoto/Entertainment Software Rating Board/AP Images, 33; Denis Paquin, file/AP Images, 36; Gerald Herbert/AP Images, 39, 45

CONTENTS

CHAPTER ONE

A New Rating

J ust remember three rules. Don't get the cute, furry little Mogwai wet. Don't let bright light shine on him. And above all, do not feed the Mogwai after midnight. What happened when Billy fed the Mogwai after midnight? Gremlins. The small green monsters terrorized the town of Kingston Falls. They broke things, caused car wrecks, and even killed Mrs. Deagle. Billy, his mom, and his friend

The soft, cuddly Mogwai turned into evil creatures in the movie *Gremlins*.

Kate tracked down and destroyed the gremlins. The worst gremlin launched a final attack on Billy with a crossbow and a chainsaw. But the gremlin was finally killed by the sunlight.

The movie was *Gremlins*. It was one of the smash hits of 1984. But the nasty critters fueled a public debate. How much screen violence should kids see? *Gremlins* was rated PG. That rating was created by the Motion Picture Association of America (MPAA). In June 1984, there were two ratings options for this movie: PG or R. The R rating would stop children under 17

In 2012, high school student Katy Butler brought boxes of petitions to the MPAA asking for a ratings change to the movie *Bully*.

from seeing the movie. *Gremlins* was not made for adult audiences. But was it okay for all children to see? Or was it too violent for young kids?

Many people thought it was too violent for children. The solution was to make a new rating. The PG-13 rating was created in July 1984. The rating warned parents not to let children under 13 see the movie. The PG-13 rating is still used today. In fact, it was the rating that *Harry Potter and the Deathly Hallows (Part One)* carried in 2010.

A mom checks her son's video games to see if they are right for his age.

What Are Ratings?

Ratings are categories for movies, television shows, video games, and mobile and online content. They warn parents about what is shown on screen. Often ratings are based on age groups. Ratings are not laws. They are a way that the media polices itself. The ratings are created and given by private organizations. Ratings are based on how much violence, sexual

Films	Television	Video Games, Mobile, and Online Downloadable Content
		EC: Early childhood, three, and older
	TV-Y: All children TV-Y7: Directed to older children TV-Y7-FV: Directed to older children, Fantasy Violence	E: Everyone, six and older
G: General audiences	TV-G: General audience	
PG: Parental Guidance suggested	PG: Parental Guidance suggested	E 10+: Everyone, ten and up
PG-13: Parents strongly cautioned, some material unsuitable for children under 13	PG-13: Parents strongly cautioned, some material unsuitable for children under 13	T: Teen, 13 and up
R: Restricted, under 17 only with an accompanying adult	TV-MA: Mature Audience only, not suitable for under 17	M: Mature, 17 and older
NC-17: Under 17 not admitted		AO: Adults Only

Media Ratings Systems

This table shows the three different media ratings systems. Read through the three types of ratings. How do they compare to the way that the ratings are explained in the text? Are they the same or different?

content, drug use, or offensive language are used in media.

The Issues of Ratings

Ratings provide information. People can make their own decisions using that information. Ideas about what is right or wrong change between people and over time. Ratings also change over time. And there is a limited number of ratings for each type of media.

Some people believe ratings are a form of censorship. What is okay for one 11-year-old may not be okay for another. Families also have different values and different thoughts about what their children should see. People may not always think a rating is right for their family.

Parents have different opinions about what their children should or should not see at movie theaters.

Ratings bring up many questions. Are ratings necessary? Do they inform audiences? Or do they limit content? Should children see some but not all content? And who should decide what children should see? These questions have been asked for decades. They are what led to the first set of parental guidance ratings in early Hollywood films.

Selznick International
Rebecca
Laurence
OLIVIER
Joan
FONTAINE
DIRECTED BY
HITCHCOCK

CHAPTER TWO

The First Ratings

In the novel *Rebecca* by Daphne du Maurier (1938), a murderer gets away with killing his wife and marries again. But director Alfred Hitchcock's movie changed an important detail in his *Rebecca* (1940). The husband does not kill his wife. She trips and hits her head. In the movie, the husband is innocent of murder.

A poster for the dark romance *Rebecca*, directed by Alfred Hitchcock and starring Laurence Olivier and Joan Fontaine

Rebecca won the Academy Award for Best Picture of 1940. But why was that detail changed? The MPAA was formed in 1922. In 1930 the MPAA created its first type of film ratings system. It was the Hays Code. It contained a list of rules for approving or disapproving movies. One of the rules was that a man could not murder someone and get away with it on film. If Alfred Hitchcock had not made a plot change, the movie would not have been approved. A movie that was disapproved would not be shown in many public theaters.

The Hays Code

The Hays Code was the MPAA's response to the public. Many wanted Hollywood movies to be censored by the government. Movies were showing

William Hays addresses the National Association of Broadcasters meeting on July 12, 1939.

things that some groups found to be indecent. William Hays, MPAA president, set a list of moral guidelines to judge movies. The code was a way for Hollywood to police itself.

The code had three general principles. It also added an older MPAA list of 36 "Don'ts" and "Be Carefuls."

The three general principles were:

1. No picture should be made that lowered the moral standards of those who saw it.

2. Correct standards of life should be shown.

3. Natural or human law should not be made fun of, and the story should not make criminals look good.

All three general principles have aspects that can be debated. The code had strict rules for how movies could show dancing, religion, and treatment of the US flag. The Hays Code also did not allow interracial couples on screen. That meant an African-American person could not kiss or date a white person in a movie. Many states at the time had laws against the marriage of whites with African Americans.

The Hays Code was used for 38 years. But the code started to seem outdated after World War II (1939–1945). Ideas about what was right and wrong in society were changing. People expected to be able to see different things in movies too.

Frank Sinatra, *middle*, plays cards in a scene from *The Man with the Golden Arm.*

In 1955 singer and actor Frank Sinatra was in a film that did not get code approval. It was *The Man with the Golden Arm*. Sinatra played a drug addict in the film. It was shown in a few theaters and received good reviews. Sinatra was even nominated for an Academy Award. This and other movies made the Hays Code seem old-fashioned.

Movie Ratings Now

Jack Valenti became the president of the MPAA in 1966. He changed the ratings system in 1968. He thought the Hays Code was a form of censorship. Valenti wanted a ratings system that would serve as a warning to viewers and parents. Today the MPAA ratings are enforced by theaters across the United States. Many theaters require a valid form of identification to prove that the person buying a ticket for an R-rated film is at least 17 years old unless with a parent.

Rating *Saving Private Ryan*

Director Steven Spielberg's film *Saving Private Ryan* is set in France during World War II. The MPAA rating is R. It has intense war violence and language. But other countries have their own ratings systems. The same movie can have many different ratings around the world. For example, in France *Saving Private Ryan* has a G rating.

Teens now see more violence in movies compared to 28 years ago. This is called "ratings creep." In an article, authors Dan Romer and Patrick E. Jamieson wrote:

> For example, a 13 year old today could see a movie like Mission Impossible 2 (2000) with intense gun and fist fighting, but in the years before 1985, prior to the introduction of the PG-13 category, the same 13-year-old would not have been allowed to view a movie with comparable explicit violence such as the R rated movie Magnum Force (1974), or even an R rated movie with less explicit violence such as 48 Hours (1982), unless he or she was accompanied by a parent or other adult. . . .
>
> The repeated exposure of youth to potentially harmful content is a serious public health concern. Extensive research has shown that repeated exposure to explicit media violence can increase violent behavior.

Source: Dan Romer and Patrick E. Jamieson. "Under MPAA's Rating System, PG-13 Movies Contain Increasingly Violent Content." The Annenberg Public Policy Center of the University of Pennsylvania. April 8, 2010. Web. Accessed June 23, 2012.

Back It Up

The author of this passage is using evidence to support a point. Write a paragraph describing the point the author is making. Then write down two or three pieces of evidence the author uses to make the point.

CHAPTER THREE

Rating Television

The animated *Yu-Gi-Oh!* series shows cartoon heroes fighting monsters. It was made for children and is rated TV-Y7. But a later version of the show has a different rating. The 5D version is rated TV-Y7-FV. The FV stands for fantasy violence. Both ratings are for the same age group, but they are different. The amount of violence separates them.

Yu-Gi-Oh! figures depict scenes from the cartoons.

A New Code

The National Association of Radio and Television Broadcasters (NARTB) made the first television rules in 1951. The rules worked like the Hays Code for movies. The code was called the Code of Practices for Television Broadcasters.

One section of the code was about responsibility toward children. It stated that violence and sexuality should not be shown. Kidnappings could not be shown, either. Children's programs and daytime television had to comply with the code.

Not everyone agreed with the rules, though. In 1982 a court case

A Guest in the Home

The first television code described television as being a guest in the home. It stated that television was seen and heard in every type of American home. These homes had children and adults of different faiths, races, ages, and educational backgrounds. The code stated that television had a responsibility to keep that audience in mind.

In 1951, a family watches the children's show *Kukla, Fran and Ollie.*

challenged the code. The court decided in the *United States v. National Association of Broadcasters* that the code was illegal. Use of the code was stopped in 1982. A new code was written in 1990.

In 1996 President Bill Clinton signed the Telecommunications Act into law. It encouraged stations to develop a ratings system for television shows. Before a ratings system was put in place, a survey was taken in 1996 to see what parents thought of it. Researchers asked 1,207 parents about the ratings. A majority of the parents wanted a ratings

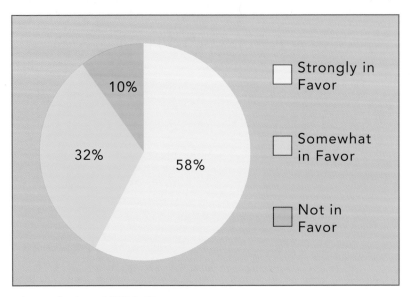

Results of the 1996 Survey

This pie chart shows the results of the 1996 survey taken on the issue of parental guidance ratings for television. Is the paragraph on pages 23–24 or the chart easier to read and understand? How is the information in the chart and paragraph similar? How is it different?

system. A small number of parents were not in favor. The result of the survey was that most parents were in support of the ratings.

The current TV Parental Guidelines were set by three organizations in 1997: the National Association of Broadcasters, the National Cable & Telecommunications Association, and the MPAA. Unlike movies, the makers of the programs rate television shows.

President Clinton holds a V-chip at the Library of Congress in Washington, where he signed the Telecommunications Act.

The V-Chip

The V-chip is technology that is used to block channels on televisions. The rating system can be enforced with this technology. The V-chip lets parents block certain shows on their televisions. All televisions made after 2000 with 13-inch (33 cm) or larger screens must have V-chip technology by law.

Resistance to Ratings

Not all television networks adopted the ratings, such as Black Entertainment Television and NBC. Some networks apply their own television ratings. They rate their own programs and sometimes rate older movies that do not have MPAA ratings. This means different networks can give the same movie a different rating. Ratings vary from network to network.

University of Michigan Research Scientist Leonard Eron was with President Clinton when he signed the V-chip law. Eron has researched the causes of violent behavior in young children since 1960. A 1996 *Michigan Today* article was about Eron's thoughts of the V-chip:

> *Eron [is doubtful about] the v-chip's ability to make much of a difference. "It's a step in the right direction," he says, "but a parent has to be concerned, and has to be available to do it. The v-chip will have some effect, but it doesn't solve the problem, not with two working parents, single-parent families and, frankly, a lot of parents who don't give a darn."*
>
> Source: Jeff Mortimer. *"Chipping Away at Violence."* Michigan Today. June 1996. Web. Accessed September 8, 2012.

What's the Big Idea?

Take a close look at Eron's quote in this interview. What is his main idea? What evidence is used to support his point? Come up with a few sentences showing how Eron uses two or three pieces of evidence to support his main point.

CHAPTER FOUR

Rating Other Media

The video games *Call of Duty 4: Modern Warfare* and *Left 4 Dead* have a few things in common. They are described as "first-person shooter" video games. The player uses a fake weapon to shoot at targets in the game. The targets may look like humans or zombies. Those human-like figures can be harmed or killed. The two games could be labeled as "violent video games." That label would have made

The *Call of Duty* video game sets a war scene where players can shoot at human characters.

Violence in Video Games

Some people believe that violence in video games leads to violence in real life. That is what sparked the desire to have ratings for video games. But some research shows that there is no link between youth violence and video games. According to Massachusetts Institute of Technology Professor Henry Jenkins, many studies that link the two have been shown to have problems with their research methods. Jenkins states that most kids who play video games do not commit criminal acts.

them illegal for minors to buy in California after 2005.

New Law in California

On October 7, 2005, Governor Arnold Schwarzenegger signed a bill making it illegal in California to sell violent video games to anyone under 18 years old. Video games labeled as being violent had to display a large sticker with the number 18 on them.

Anyone who broke this law had to pay up to a $1,000 fine. Less than two weeks later, the Video Software Dealers Association filed a lawsuit trying to stop the law.

California Governor Arnold Schwarzenegger fought to make violent video games harder for children to buy.

In 2007 Judge Ronald M. Whyte heard the case. He ruled against the law. The judge believed that the law was unconstitutional. It violated the First Amendment right to free speech. Governor Schwarzenegger appealed this decision. The appeal went to the US Supreme Court in 2010. Its justices upheld the 2007 ruling. The justices suggested that

EVERYONE **10+**

™

E 10+

Cartoon Violence
Mild Lyrics

ESRB CONTENT RATING   **www.esrb.org**

The ESRB introduced a new video game rating category, E10+ (Everyone 10 and older), in 2005.

a voluntary rating system for video games was an effective way to warn parents about violence in video games.

The ESRB Ratings Now

With the rise in video games and mobile and online content, the entertainment industry decided a ratings system would be useful. The Entertainment Software Rating Board (ESRB) was created in 1994. The ESRB made a rating system for video games. It then decided to police the makers and sellers to make sure they put the ratings on the games. Buyers and users of these games could then choose for themselves.

Many large companies that sell video games, such as Best Buy, Target, and GameStop, have joined with the ESRB to enforce the ratings. When a minor attempts to buy a video game rated M or AO, the sales employees can refuse to sell the game. Just as

EXPLORE ONLINE

The focus in Chapter Four is the rating of video games and online and mobile content. The PBS Web site below focuses on the violence in video games. As you know, every source is different. How is the information given in the Web site different from the information in this chapter? What information is the same? How do the two sources present information differently? What can you learn from this Web site?

Do You Know What Video Games Your Children Are Playing?

www.pbs.org/kcts/videogamerevolution/impact/violence.html

a movie theater may enforce the MPAA ratings, many video game stores enforce the ESRB ratings.

The ESRB joined with The Wireless Association (CTIA) to rate apps for phones or mobile devices. In 2012 the rating was shown on certain digital stores before a user downloaded the app. The buyer can choose whether or not to buy that app based on the rating.

These ratings vary among companies, though. Apple and Google do not use the ESRB ratings. They have their own sets of ratings. The different ratings systems can be confusing to buyers. They must figure out what each set of ratings means before making a decision about the content.

Apple and Google

When the CTIA announced its ratings system in 2011, Apple and Google already had their own ratings. They rejected the CTIA ratings system. Instead, Apple uses age ratings. Google uses maturity level ratings. These two companies hold the largest share of this type of media market.

Apple has its own ratings system for its apps.

CHAPTER FIVE

The Case of Ratings

When industries regulate themselves, there are both benefits and problems. It is good for the maker of the media. Ratings can be specific to the media they were designed for. And the ratings organizations can easily adjust their own ratings. Viewers can use the ratings as they wish. It is a form of information for parents. They can make informed decisions about what their children see.

MPAA President Jack Valenti spoke during a news conference at the National Press Club on December 19, 1996, where he announced the new television ratings system.

But media viewers and users must know and understand several different ratings systems. It can be confusing to viewers. A show that has a low rating on one station may have a higher rating on another. For movies, some consider the ratings to be a form of censorship. If the MPAA gives a movie a higher rating, fewer people will be able to see it. And some movie theaters may not show the movie at all. A rating can stop a movie from reaching a large audience. Its message, such as the one in the movie *Bully*, will not be heard. And in the case of *Bully*, younger audiences may have been most affected by its message.

Common Sense Media

Books do not have ratings, but Common Sense Media uses a traffic light system to rate all types of media, including books. It rated *The Hunger Games* book green. That means it is okay for 12-year-olds. *The Hunger Games* movie is rated PG-13 by the MPAA. Common Sense Media suggests that the movie is okay for 16- to 17-year-olds.

According to a study by Common Sense Media, approximately 40 percent of two- to four-year-olds have used a smartphone, tablet, or video iPod.

Alternative Ratings

Some specialized groups create their own ratings based on shared values. Focus on the Family, for example, reviews media for children based on how well the media upholds Christian values. Common Sense Media has a color-coded traffic light rating system for all media, including books. The reviewer rates each product and parents and kids do too.

The Common Sense Media's Web site shows the results of all three ratings as well as any rating given by a major rating system, such as the MPAA. These kinds of groups offer more information to parents. Based on their values, parents may find them useful in making their own decisions. And these independent ratings systems are not connected with the makers of the media. The ratings reflect the values of the organizations that created them. These organizations are not concerned with how much money a show or movie makes.

Future Ratings

Media is changing constantly. New types of media and ways to view media are being introduced every day. And children use technology

Using the V-chip

A 2007 Kaiser Family Foundation study found that people aren't really using the V-chip in their televisions. Only 43 percent of the people in the study knew that they had V-chips in their televisions. And just 16 percent were using the V-chip. Most in the study did not understand the meaning of the ratings.

and media at younger and younger ages. There are also stations with programs just for children. Parental ratings may be outdated due to these changes. As media and its audiences change, parental guidance ratings may have to be examined again. The ratings will surely evolve into the future.

FURTHER EVIDENCE

There is quite a bit of information about alternative ratings in Chapter Five. It covered some different groups that make their own media ratings. But if you could pick out the main point of the chapter, what would it be? What evidence was given to support that point? Visit the Web site below to learn more about independent ratings. Choose a quote from the Web site that relates to this chapter. Does this quote support the author's main point? Does it make a new point? Write a few sentences explaining how the quote you found relates to this chapter.

Are the Common Sense Media Ratings a Better MPAA Alternative?

blog.moviefone.com/2010/03/22/are-the-common-sense-media-ratings-a-better-mpaa-alternative/

IMPORTANT DATES

1922

The MPAA is formed.

1930

The Hays Code becomes the ratings standard for movies.

1951

The Code of Practices for Television Broadcasters is adopted to rate television shows.

1994

The Entertainment Software Rating Board is created to rate video games, online content, and online privacy settings.

1996

The Telecommunications Act is signed into law on February 8.

1997

The TV Parental Guideline System is created.

1968

The MPAA movie ratings system is created.

1982

The United States v. National Association of Broadcasters case challenges the television code and its use is stopped.

1984

The PG-13 rating is created for movies.

2000

The Telecommunications Act requires that all television sets with 13-inch (33 cm) screens or larger must be V-chip enabled.

2005

Governor Arnold Schwarzenegger signs a bill on October 7 making it illegal in California to sell violent video games to anyone under 18.

2011

The Supreme Court rules that stopping the sale of violent video games to minors was unconstitutional.

Why Do I Care?

Media is something we all use or see every day. Come up with two or three ways parental guidance ratings connect with your life. Do your parents or guardians allow you to see movies that are rated PG-13 or higher? Do you know what the ratings are for the television shows that you watch? Do you have parental controls on your television or computer?

Another View

There are many sources online and in your library about parental guidance ratings. Ask a librarian or other adult to help you find a reliable source on the parental guidance ratings. Compare what you learn in this new source with what you have found out in this book. Then write a short essay comparing and contrasting the new source's view of parental guidance ratings to the ideas in this book. How are they different? How are they similar? Why do you think they are different or similar?

Surprise Me

The history and use of parental guidance ratings can be interesting and surprising. What two or three facts about parental guidance ratings did you find most surprising? Write a few sentences about each fact. Why did you find them surprising?

Say What?

Learning about parental guidance ratings can mean learning a lot of new vocabulary. Can you find five words in this book that you've never seen or heard? First find out the meanings of those words. Then write down the meanings in your own words. After that try to use each word in a new sentence.

GLOSSARY

appeal
ask for a decision made by a court of law to be changed

censorship
the blocking of information

comply
meet or obey certain terms

documentary
type of film showing real life

indecent
unpleasant, rude, or shocking

interracial
involving different races

expletive
swear word

media
art or communications made for us to watch, read, or hear

moral
a belief or set of beliefs about what is right or wrong

survey
questions asked of a group of people about their opinions on a subject

trailers
short movie clips made to advertise a movie

unconstitutional
not keeping with the laws set forth in the constitution of a state or country

LEARN MORE

Books

Allman, Toney. *Media Violence*. Yankton, SD: Erickson Press, 2007.

Magoon, Kekla. *Media Censorship*. Edina, MN: ABDO Publishing, 2010.

Senker, Cath. *Violence*. Mankato, MN: Smart Apple Media, 2010.

Web Links

To learn more about parental guidance ratings, visit ABDO Publishing Company online at **www.abdopublishing.com**. Web sites about parental guidance ratings are featured on our Book Links page. These links are routinely monitored and updated to provide the most current information available.

Visit **www.mycorelibrary.com** for free additional tools for teachers and students.

INDEX

ABOUT THE AUTHOR

Casie Hermansson teaches English at Pittsburg State
University. She writes fiction and nonfiction for
young readers.